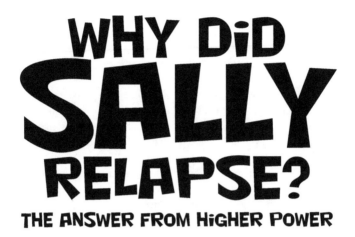

WHY DiD SALLY RELAPSE?

THE ANSWER FROM HiGHER POWER

DARLENE M. GRANT

WESTBOW
PRESS®
A DIVISION OF THOMAS NELSON
& ZONDERVAN

This book is a work of non-fiction. Unless otherwise noted, the author
and the publisher make no explicit guarantees as to the accuracy of
the information contained in this book and in some cases, names
of people and places have been altered to protect their privacy.

WestBow Press books may be ordered through booksellers or by contacting:

WestBow Press
A Division of Thomas Nelson & Zondervan
1663 Liberty Drive
Bloomington, IN 47403
www.westbowpress.com
1 (866) 928-1240

Because of the dynamic nature of the Internet, any web addresses or
links contained in this book may have changed since publication and
may no longer be valid. The views expressed in this work are solely those
of the author and do not necessarily reflect the views of the publisher,
and the publisher hereby disclaims any responsibility for them.

Any people depicted in stock imagery provided by Getty Images are
models, and such images are being used for illustrative purposes only.
Certain stock imagery © Getty Images.

Scripture taken from the King James Version of the Bible.

ISBN: 978-1-9736-6157-3 (sc)
ISBN: 978-1-9736-6158-0 (hc)
ISBN: 978-1-9736-6156-6 (e)

Library of Congress Control Number: 2019906872

Print information available on the last page.

WestBow Press rev. date: 06/10/2019

ACKNOWLEDGMENTS

A special thank you to my mother, Jean Grant, who I have admired and has always been my inspiration.

Thank you, Kimberly Milton, for your patience and support, since we were kids living at home. Minister Joseph Smith, for your lectures and support, I thank you. Pearl Bennett, thank you for your loving-kindness and nonjudgmental heart. Valerie Miller, also for listening to me. Of course, thank you, a thousand times, Willie White. A special thank-you to Arnold White and (Six) Lawrence Kindel, who are no longer with me but went to great lengths to help and support me. Thank you, Pastor Harry Ward, for listening to me and for your advice.

Thank you, **SALLY**.

CONTENTS

INTRODUCTION

I feel sad whenever I hear anyone refer to an object as their higher power. To some the higher power can be regarded to be a fleeting object, like a light switch or their significant other or latest relationship. They have declared it so because they don't know where their help comes from. I think it's a sad commentary to feel there is nothing larger than yourself that you can run to for refuge.

I understand many people still do not know who they worship. I thought to myself, *Well, I've got to tell them. I will tell them who he is and what he requires of them, and their lives will be enriched, too.*

Why Did Sally Relapse is a look at addiction through my experiences and from my spiritual viewpoint, focusing on the relationship between the addict and the higher power. My relationship with my higher power is the catalyst to my successful recovery. This is a step-by-step guide to God's help for the addict.

Only God, a power greater than man, who created man, can restore man to himself before addiction.

Only he can break the addictive power of crack cocaine, heroin, opioids, and methamphetamines.

The power of addiction is satanic, and there are demons that work in atmospheres where drug use is present. Therefore, God is staging an intervention by extending his liberty of freedom from addiction. He is also simultaneously restoring the power of choice so we may freely choose him. He does this so he can graft us in. Without this intervention from God, addicts would die in their addiction.

This power requires a relationship. Addicts can only choose to use. God has leveled the playing field so we can find freedom and live the lives we are called to and walk in the liberty we are called to.

The question of why Sally relapsed will be addressed. Who the higher power is will be revealed. And you will hear a message from the higher power that gives the keys to freedom from addiction.

PART I

CHAPTER 1

The Abyss

Each spirit has its own personality and is known by its evil.

One hundred people die every day from drug overdoses. Six million people with an addiction also have a mental disorder.

These are the numbers of Americans addicted to different substances: tobacco, 40 million; alcohol, 18 million;

marijuana: 4.2 million; painkillers, 1.8 million; cocaine, eight hundred twenty-one thousand; and heroin, four hundred twenty-six thousand.

Drugs go through cycles—in the 1980s and early 90s, the use of crack cocaine surged. In the early 2000s, meth made from pseudoephedrine, the decongestant in drugstore products poured out of domestic labs.

In 2005 Congressed passed the Combat Methamphetamine Act, which puts pseudoephedrine behind the counter and limits amount of grams per customer in 30 day period and requires pharmacist to track sales.

More than sixty-four thousand Americans died from drug overdoses in 2016, including illicit drugs and prescription opioids. That number has nearly doubled in a decade.[1]

1 Hedegaard H, Warner M, Menino A. M, Drug Overdose Deaths in the United States. 1999-2016. National Center for Health Statistics. Data Brief, No. 294. Hyattsville, M.D. National Center for Health Statistics, 2017.

---

[1] The Center for Disease Control and Prevention.

In 2016 948,000 Americans reported using heroin in past year. This number is on the rise. This trend is driven by young adults aged 18-25. One hundred seventy thousand people started heroin use in 2016 nearly doubled the number of people in 2006, (90,000).[2]

Cocaine use has gone down in the last few years. In 2013 the number of current users aged 12 or older was 1.5 million. This number is lower than in 2002 to 2007 (ranging from 2.0 million to 2.4 million)[3]

In 2011, there were approximately 20.6 million people in the United States over the age of twelve with an addiction, excluding tobacco.

National Death Rates / National Institute on Drug Abuse

Drug overdose death rose from 16,849 in 1999 to 70,237 in 2017. More than 70,200 Americans died from drug overdoses in 2017, including illicit drugs and prescription

---

[2] National Institute on Drug Abuse
Drug facts/heroin/national institute on drug abuse(NIDA)
https://www.drugabuse.gov/publication/drugfact/heroin
[3] Drug/Fact: Cocaine/National Institute on Drug Abuse (NIDA)
https://wwwdugeabuse.gov/publications/drugfacts/cacaine

opioids—a 2-fold increase in a decade. Overdose Death Rates / National Institute on Drug Abuse (NIDA)

https://www.drugabuse.gov/related-topics/trends-statistics/overdose-death rates. (Source: Center DC WONDER)

Regular marijuana use can lead to respiratory cancer.

Cannabis Use and Risk of Lung Cancer: A Case – Control Study

The results of the present study indicate that long-term cannabis use increases the risk of lung cancer in young adults.[4]

Every imaginable evil lives in the abyss. It has varying degrees of madness that have no bottom. Oftentimes in one's life span, devastation can sweep through a nation or a generation.

---

[4] European Respiratory journal
Flagship Scientific Journal of ERS
Cannabis Use and Risk of Lung Cancer: A Case-Control Study
S. Aldington, J. Harwood, B. Cox, M. Weatherall, L. Beckert, A. Hansell, A. Pritchard, G. Robinson, R. Beasley. European Respiratory journal 2008 31: 280-286; DOI:10 1183/09031936 00665707

Crack cocaine is one of those evils. The driving force behind the addiction is pure evil himself. Crack cocaine, heroin, meth, prescription painkillers, and opioids, to mention a few, are evil inventions with influences from the pit.

I want to believe prescription pain medicine is a good invention. I am very appreciative that friends and family don't have to suffer in pain, but evil rises up from the use of these medications after one is addicted. What is meant for one's good can turn one into a monster.

Evil spirits dwell with addiction. Chemical dependence causes mental illness in its users. Jesus healed people with all manner of sickness, and other times he delivered those filled with evil spirits. Each spirit has its own evil and influence that you take on when you engage it. Accordingly, when you do a drug, you take on the influence of the drug and the spirit in it.

Alcohol spirits can make some people depressed, others angry, and others happy, while turning some into transients. Heroin spirits make their users vomit, nod out, or go to sleep. Cocaine spirits cause their users to become aggressive and paranoid. There are smoking demons, opioid demons, sex demons, gambling spirits, and lying spirits—and many more spirits, like fear, scheming, murderous spirits that strive to kill anyone if there's an opportune time. These spirits are in the atmosphere and in the users. When the right cocktail is present, for example, with the use of highly addictive drugs, there is arguing, scheming, and fear when drugs are running low. These spirits that are hanging around spring to life, and people can lose their lives.

CHAPTER 2

Addiction

There are spirits of addiction. These demons are here with us to ensure our destruction during drug use.

Addiction accomplishes the agenda of Satan. It robbed me of all my resources. Addicts end up in hospitals with failing organs, suffering with mental health issues, or in jail. People lose their lives because they will do anything to get drugs. Drugs are so addictive and their users want them at any cost.

It seems like drug's plagues are unleashed on the earth. These plagues are from hell. They ravish and destroy everything in their wake. It's a weapon formed against humankind. It causes the brain to malfunction, too. My brain wanted its dose of drugs and was sending me messages to that effect. My brain, once normal, had gone rogue and sought only the pleasure derived from drug use. I was aware that my brain was consumed with the scope of using, even at the cost of my death.

Like Paul, I too had wondered where my redemption would come from, and at other times, I hoped God was big enough to break the addictive power.

The State of an Addict

> *For that which I do I allow not; for what I would that do I not; but what I hate, that do I. (Romans 7:15)*

I too was weak. Addicts are powerless here, with no ability to choose.

It is not me but the power of addiction that dwelled in me.

How to perform that which is good, I find not.

I remember trying many times, but I was not able to abstain. The urge to use would be ever present.

The brain changes your mind for you. I said, "No, I'm not using today," but somehow I ended up in the backseat of the car, and the addiction was driving.

I was miserable, and I had no control. I wanted to abstain but was unable to. The addiction I hated was the drug I craved.

> I know it is not me—society says it's the disease in me. "*I find then a law, that, when I would do good, evil is present with me.*" *(Romans 7:21)*

This insatiable desire to use warred against my mind and brought me into captivity.

> *Oh, wretched man that I am! Who shall deliver me from the body of this death?* *(Romans 7:24)*

Paul said, "*I thank God through Jesus Christ our Lord*" *(Romans 7:25)*. Know your *deliverer*!

I wanted to serve God. My heart wanted to, but I couldn't because my own selfish will got in the way of his commandments. That stupid addiction was always with me. The reason I could not control my will was because the urge to use was always there. It was sickening. Every day I would feel that maddening desire. The addictive power was stronger than my will. It's the brain; it becomes set on one cycle, and that is using and always that one cycle. Crack cocaine was a master that ruled with an iron fist. Jesus said, *"You cannot serve two masters; you will love the one and hate the other"* *(Matthew 6:24).*

I had God, who is a jealous God, and the addiction, which comes with a takeover spirit. I hated that takeover spirit. I despised the time it demanded that I was unable to give to God and the money wasted in addiction. I hated the stronghold it had over my life. I hated the drug with all my might. I hated the embarrassment of becoming a different person, of always not having enough resources to help anyone and not measuring up to my full potential. I remember my girlfriend at work asked me why I was wearing stockings with lent beads all over them. I was an administrative secretary, after all. I couldn't very well tell her my salary was funding my crack addiction. But I did play if off as though I was unaware of the lent beads, and I thanked her for telling me.

She said, "You have a good position. You should look better." Then I was embarrassed.

Whatever I couldn't defeat by my own means, I learned to give it to God. So I had to put my addiction in God's hands, and I waited for my appointed time—the time when God would set me free.

The addiction must first be removed before I or any addict can serve God. I can accept God and put my hope in him that one day he will take the addiction away, but I cannot serve God with my mind and body until the addiction is removed. Addicts can't serve God. That is why God has staged an intervention by offering his liberty and giving them their power of choice back. When I was addicted, I thought about using. Life revolved around substance abuse. I came to God and asked for forgiveness of my sins. I trusted God to remove the addiction. But until the addiction was removed, I sought help to abstain from using. Help was available.

The best way for me to demystify the hold crack cocaine had on me was to liken it to a living, breathing spouse.

The additive spirit is in the drug. This spouse is beyond dysfunctional because this spouse is greedy and cares about nothing but thinking for you and driving you to spend more and more money. It wants more and more of your time and attention—satisfying nothing but your urge to use. This spirit wants to cut you off from family and friends because they interfere with your ability to use. And you—well, you become henpecked, the obedient slave. This spouse wants you to love it more than life itself, and you will until you begin to hate it. You soon realize it won't be so easy getting rid of this spouse. Spending time with others, including your employer, will be scrutinized. This spouse is manipulative and jealous. This spouse is never satisfied and will take over your lust for life and become your motivation to wake up and get through the day. Instead of supporting you, it will destroy everything you stand for. Your principles will be trampled underfoot. And it will expect you to steal for it. Family will recoil when they see you coming because you look like the walking dead, like you never sleep or like a zombie. Family won't know how to help you. You will find it impossible to be accountable and loyal. Intimacy will become nonexistent because you will lose your ability to interact with a real person. Your drug spouse, as you spend more time with it, will destroy your sense of what is normal and sanctioned by God. It is the nature of the spirit. And then, after that, you will have a heart attack or some other organ will fail and your appointment with death will arrive. And I prayed God would get me to my appointed time before my appointment with death.

I've turned down invitations to go out with friends because I feared my drug spouse would cause me to cancel anyway. Crack cocaine has dominion over the addict until God removes it, as though it were a spouse because when it calls you answer and it has a central part of your life.

God broke my addiction, not me. I tried, and I couldn't do it. Therefore, I am giving God the highest honor. He is the head of my life. I do nothing without considering his commandments first.

How naive it is to forget God, whose liberty you walk in. I choose his liberty because I choose to live holy and on good ground, safe from the world of a relapsed lifestyle.

Jesus said, "You can do nothing without me" (John 5:15). So we have to be connected to him. Believe me, I don't want to do anything without him.

The second time I asked God to liberate me from drugs, he didn't give me his liberty. He gave me an appointed time, and I had to wait for my appointed time with patience. I went and met as a group with others who were similarly afflicted, and we had discussions and encouraged each other. We lifted one another up and prayed together.

I realized that when we met from different nationalities and religious backgrounds, when we prayed, each one to their own God, to be clean from drugs, we were inviting our gods into the recovery process. However, it was my God who was showing up and permeating the room with his presence. It was my God who was breaking the chains of bondage as addicts were being set free, and others were getting clean days in.

And there were days when we were able to stay clean. I needed God's' plan for my life to know what direction to go. I continued my life as it was but incorporated his will and commandments into my daily living, and that is what turned my life in a different direction. I was not able to direct my own life, and neither did I want to. I would much rather rely on him.

We need God's plan for our lives. This will help us stay clean and give us a new direction. I can do nothing without him, so I walk in his liberty and focus to accomplish the things he gave me to do in my own life. These works are planted in me just as your works are planted in you.

I had to be connected to God by his spirit to stay clean. His spirit had to dwell in me to keep the satanic power of addiction at bay. When God extends his liberty to you and you find yourself free from drugs and you don't know what to make of it, it is a miracle. It is a gift from God almighty extending his freedom to you and simultaneously giving you your power of choice, so you can freely choose him. If you don't choose God and make him the head of your life, another opportunity to do so may not come for years, and in the meantime you could be using.

Every time you ask God to take the addiction away, there is a time set that God will make it happen. That is divine timing or an appointed time. Whatever it is, it is in his timing.

So when God shows up with your freedom from drugs that you have been hoping and praying for, only he knows the day and *hour because "he worketh all things after the counsel of his own will" (Ephesians 1:11)*. He's not going to see if you've been going to church or group.

That day will be etched in your memory for years to come or forever.

That is the liberty God extended to me. I was delivered, and everyone saw that I was. When I relapsed, all I kept hearing was, "Why did Sally relapse?" Even I wondered, *why did I relapse? "Whom the Son frees is free indeed."* I had to understand this mystery.

I hated the drugs. I told God, "If you don't get this drug out of my life, I will die. I cannot do it myself or I would have done it long ago. Lord, I can't do it without you. How long do I have to wait?"

I remember asking God to remember me when I was eleven years old—when I first got saved. I asked the Lord to remember how close we were and any good I had done and have mercy on me and save me from this life of addiction, rather than let me die.

I could not perform the simplest of tasks, like paying the bills, not to mention paying them on time. Having lunch with a friend was something only to dream about because I didn't dare commit to anything that would take me away from my greedy spouse. This greedy spouse can be anywhere and could call without a phone. It is a war against the mind.

Family and friends don't understand how their loved ones can be ruled by a drug and wreck their entire lives. Well, the craving is strong and has the strength of a satanic beast.

When you go swimming on a hot summer day, eat your favorite ice cream, or read that favorite book, this activates the brain's reward system, but you don't become addicted to it. You can let it go and pick it up at a later time.

However, when drugs are used recreationally, they become addictive to the brain's pleasure center. The brain then wants pleasure nonstop, even if it causes the user to die. This is a side effect of addiction.

PART II

CHAPTER 3

Building Spirituality

The most intimate relationship you can have with your Higher Power is to be his bride—be married to him, *"that ye may bring forth fruit unto God"* (Romans 7:14). In this marriage, God requires that all of us who are married to him work. But I longed to do his will, and I desired to do good works and bear good fruit. I desire to do his will on earth.

Get spiritual with him. How else will you know who you are married to? I am married to him in righteousness and he shows me justice. I am married to him in judgment and he is compassionate with me. He is mine in lovingkindness and in mercy. I am faithful because he gives me unfailing love. I needed a personal relationship with him. I had to experience him. I am connected with him on the vine and nothing can separate me from his love. When I keep his commandments, I obligate him to me. I can ask whatsoever I will, and at the appointed time, he will do it. And he will see my dreams comes true because his will is my will.

I needed him—but I also wanted him. I wanted to impress him. I wanted to be his bride. I needed this marriage to happen right away because I was desperate for his love. I wanted my gown to be spotless—pure white. I knew only he could remove the stain, the spot, the blemish, the wrinkle, the *addiction*. I knew that where he is, freedom is. I was becoming obsessed with him because I knew where he is, the chains of bondage will fall away. I knew that powers obeyed him. I heard of others who had years of clean time, and I wanted the same for myself.

I set out to make him mine. I began meditating on every word he spoke and everything that was said about him. He became all I could think of, and I wanted him to move for me. How could I affect him? I needed him, and I wanted him just as badly. I needed him now in real time, though, not in appointed time or divine timing. I had to know what he required that I should do. It was then that I decided to make his will my will. When his will becomes my will, my will is his will.

As in any relationship where there is constant communication, we began to develop intimacy. I strived to be near him. And I searched the scriptures to learn how to know him. Spirituality is holy intimacy, some type of relationship between God and me.

We are close because I am known by him. His spirit communes with my spirit. I began to talk to him about the intimate details of my life and my aspirations. I began to confess my faults and praise him in our relationship. Oftentimes I sang to Him in the confines of my home— just me and the Lord alone at home. He taught me how to love and reverence him.

My higher power required that I be married to him to bring forth good works. To build spirituality, my higher power required that I should keep his commandments. So I began to read the New Testament so I could keep his word in my heart. When you walk in this liberty, you will feel his joy. I began to feel his joy. He required that I should be patient and wait on him. That kept me focused on him. Waiting on God is the absolute best way to learn patience, and it builds spirituality. I became dependent upon him. That was how I began to feel connected to God. I needed my Father to fix my life, and he did.

It was also a relief to cast my cares on him. And when I prayed, I knew he heard me. I knew he heard me because he gave me his peace and I was keeping his commandments and confessing my sin. There was nothing untoward between us. However, I don't profess to be perfect. I continue to confess my sins. When I confess to him, I believe that he throws it into the sea of forgetfulness and he can't remember it anymore. He literally empties the fruits of his Spirit into my spirit. And I feel his Spirit communing with mine.

So listen to your spirit and really hear what God is saying in your spirit. Always keep track of what God is saying to you and incorporate it into your daily life, if you can. (Write it in a journal so you don't forget God's plans and directions to you.)

Building this relationship with the higher power is your responsibility. To learn of him, read the four gospels.

For as I passed by, and beheld your devotions, I found an altar with this inscription, "TO THE UNKNOWN GOD," whom ye ignorantly worship, him declare I unto you. (Acts 17:23)

CHAPTER 4

Your Higher Power

*All power both in heaven and in Earth has
been given unto him. (Matthew 28:18)*

He is part of a holy trinity: God the Father, God the Son,
and God the Holy Spirit.

I can experience the God of my sobriety in any one of
these three entities.

God the Father is the first person of the godhead, the Creator of the universe. God is a sovereign being, in complete control.

Experience him as your father because Jesus said, "*Ye have not received the spirit of bondage to fear; but ye have received the Spirit of adoption, whereby we cry, Abba (our) Father*" (Romans 8:15).

I could feel the adoption going through. I felt it in my spirit. I'm a sensitive, intuitive person, and I did feel the adoption literally going through.

He is also the Gardener.

God the Son is the second person of the godhead—Jesus, the higher power.

> *He was born of the seed of David according to the flesh, and declared to be the Son of God with power, according to the will of God by the resurrection from the dead. (Romans 1:3–4)*

Jesus wants our joy to remain by giving us our hearts' desires. Yes, I want this friendship.

He gave us a gift: the Comforter.

He prays for us.

Jesus touches my heart and I do his will, and I know I am his sister and mother.

God the Holy Spirit is the third person of the godhead. He is a spirit—invisible, like the wind. *You will feel him and hear him, but you cannot tell where he came from or where he is going (John 3:8).*

He will put in your spirit directions from God. He will also pull from your spirit the word of God when you need it.

That's why it is important that I read the word and get it in my heart so the Holy Spirit can bring it to my mind when I am weak.

Be strong in your faith in Jesus. He will take your addiction and put it under your feet, and he will give you an abundant life. The people around you will literally be amazed at how blessed your life has become. God will propel you to where he wants you to be in life. He will get you there!

The quickest way to get God's attention, I find, is to keep his commandments. I have chosen to live my life within the confines of good ground. Keep that mind-set and you won't relapse. Don't be afraid when you have time on your hands and you don't know what to do. Follow your spirit because this is the channel through which God communicates with us. Jesus is the Good Shepard.

Jesus said, "My sheep know my voice."

God speaks to me through the soft, quiet, still voice inside me.

If you can't hear the voice God planted inside you, perhaps it is because you need to seek to be like God more. As you become spiritual, or Christlike, your inner man will begin to come forth, the person you are to become like. The inner man, the link from God to you—he is in a union with God when you accept Jesus as Lord and Savior. As you conform by learning what is written in his word, the renewing of your mind will start to take place and you will hear God's voice speaking to you, and your very nature will become like God's. You will know what behavior is offensive to God. You will start to hate your addiction and want it out of your life. You will start to change. There were even certain sin and people I did not want around me any longer.

I developed an established prayer life. Communication between God and me on a daily basis establishes a close bond, and I remember feeling friendly toward God. I felt he was another person, a friend. He will start to feel like a friend, but he said that those who do what his Father commands are his friends. Experience him as your friend. I digress. I started by just picking a time of day, seven o'clock in the morning, for example. That was my time each day to talk to God. This will become habit forming, if you practice it.

Prayer is the time to get to know the God of my deliverance. Jesus is love. He restored my soul and gave me my mind back. He saved me and made me whole. I want to show my love for him by doing whatever God would have me to do. Walk in the liberty to do his will. When we were in bondage, we could not do his will. You will want to do his will. When you follow his commandments, that is when you are allowing him to direct your life, and that is when you get presents from God. When you allow him to direct your will, he leads you into the blessings he has for you.

Experience him as your friend. Jesus said, *"Ye are my friends, if ye do whatsoever I command you"* (John 15:14). Whether Jesus speaks to you through his word or lays something on your heart for you to do, when you obey him, all will go well with you. And then you will know you've done his will and you are his friend.

Trouble Will Come

Jesus warns us like a true friend because he loves us, "that trouble will come." So maybe we can be prepared in some instances. Just because I am no longer chemically dependent does not mean trouble will not come into my life. When it does come, it will not come with the power to make me relapse. That is why Jesus warns us so that we know that nothing will separate us from him and his love. He is a great friend that we can depend on and trust. When trouble does come, it will not impact us directly because Jesus promised he would never leave us even until the end of the world. God literally gives his children the wisdom to navigate this life and gives us his power to live right and his peace to be at rest.

I pray for wisdom. I do the work that helps others and trust where God is taking my life. I am friends with

Jesus, and I cast all of my cares on him. It is another relief to my mind that I can do that.

We are using God's wisdom to make wise choices concerning our lives. We can cast our cares on him with confidence. So when trouble comes, nothing will separate us from his love, and whatever trouble comes will not be able to diminish our faith in the God of our sobriety. His spirit still dwells within me and is stronger than anything that can come against me. As long as I live my life on good ground, I will make wise decisions over my life—wisdom given to me by God himself. I accept that trouble will come, but I don't fear trouble. I am always confident because God gives me wisdom to navigate this life even while I pass through its troubles. It goes back to doing God's will and not mine, thus living on good ground and allowing God to direct my path. You will see the way and make the right choices if you follow this.

This spiritually is developed when I walk in his word. His word is spirit; the word is alive and lives in me. This is why his word has to remain in me. The word cleanses me, and his truth (his word/commandments) has the power to keep me free from addiction.

God almighty, in heaven above, promises me and everyone who keeps his commandments a visitation; he will personally manifest himself to each of us individually because we are the beloved of God (John 14:21). We who love God are the ones who keep his commandments. We are the beloved of God because we keep his commandments. Can you imagine being the beloved of God? That's having access to God. It is we who keep his commandments who have the authority to go directly before God in prayer.

If you keep his commandments, you are experiencing some blessings from God. You should be experiencing inner joy and peace. You should have a sense of the indwelling of the Holy Spirit in you. The Holy Spirit is God's gift to me and to you—to help us on the path we are to travel. When I walk in my vocation, I can feel the spirit within me and the spirit of addiction is away somewhere.

When you align your life with him, you are entitled to his blessings, and he is revealing himself to you and the direction you are to travel, awakening dreams he planted in you.

Learn the mannerism God uses with you. I remember one Sunday morning I was listening to Pastor Joel Osteen preach. He was on television, and I was many states away seated on my bed listening to him. Suddenly, after a few seconds, I became aware that God was present with me. Know his presence! It was a very different experience yet an awesome occurrence because for a moment, God and I were listening to Joel Osteen preach about him. God can be situated anywhere and hear everything people are saying about him, and for the most part, no one is the wiser.

Enter into his rest.

Welcome. Please, enter in. All are welcome. Come in and rest yourself. Give yourself a break. He wants to meet your needs. He wants to be a present help to you. Enter into his rest. Feel his loving arms. Jesus loves you so much and can give you the help your life needs. He wanted to help my life, and I allowed him to do just that. He performed miracles in my life, literally, and propelled me to a whole new level. That's what our God is capable of. He wants you to bask in the blessings he has for you. He already knows what you need and what you want because he has the answers you seek.

No more worrying about finding money to support my habit or pinching off the bill money. Finally, a whole new way of life. I gladly entered into this rest. You can only enter into his rest if you trust God and have confidence in him. If you enter in, he will give you his peace. I was tired of the world and its drug dealers and life's admonishment of me. I entered into his rest and simply followed his commandments. If you want to live a blessed life, start applying his commandments to your life and to your decisions immediately.

When you experience him as your Father, you will trust in his rest and enter in. What a relief you will feel when you give the responsibility over to him and feel the weight lifted. What responsibility, you may ask? Your life! If you enter into his rest, your burdens will be light. Your burdens will be light because you won't have any burdens—just God's will for your life, which are the dreams he planted in you.

There will be times when you will have to exercise patience as Job in the Old Testament did. In fact, patience was the biggest thing I had to learn to live with after the addiction. I waited years for God to answer some of my prayers. That is how he matures us—patience in tough times. We must prepare our part and allow God to lead.

Learn the art of praise. Can you imagine being so humble, down to earth, that you never forget to give praise to God?

In the movie *The Ten Commandments* with Charlton Heston, do you remember when the frail old Hebrew slave woman's only son dies? Mind you, she is stuck under the wheel of some apparatus and the slaves are trying to save her from being crushed under it. When they tell her as she is stuck under the wheel her son has died, her response is, "Blessed is the name of the Lord forever." She has mastered the art of praise. Can you imagine that kind of faith in God? I must remember God in all my affairs.

You will know God is leading you when he gives you his peace. You will know you are doing God's will when the vision begins to open up. You can lead a very healthy, good, and prosperous life after addiction. After addiction, life seemed to smile on me. I started painting by numbers, writing, doing a little fundraising, eating out, going to the movies, landscaping, etc.

Addiction took up hours of my day just about each day. So when it was over, my time had to be restructured. Needing to restructure my life, filling up the idle time, and realizing things don't happen overnight was the biggest hurdle. And I was always trying to enjoy the blessings in my life while enduring life's pain of always being bored.

If you truly trust God and have confidence in him, then cast your cares on him. I know your pain. When you are getting your sobriety, you are afraid to tell anyone because you don't know if it's really over. You don't believe anyone will believe you, so you keep it to yourself. Jesus blessed the broken spirited. Have faith in what God is telling you, and cast your cares on your friend. He will never leave you. But you might have to wait for your appointed time. Whatever God plants in your heart or has shown you in your future, believe in it. When God speaks to us, there is no doubt that it is him. You must think back to who it was who was speaking to you. Remember God's holy presence when he spoke to you, and then stand on your faith and relive that moment as many times as you need and keep encouraging yourself.

Remember, it is not only death that we have an appointed time for; everything is by appointment.

Even Jesus had an appointed time:

Jesus told his mother *his hour had not yet come.* (Jesus had an appointed time.) (John 2:4)

For Sarah conceived, and bore Abraham a son in his old age, at he set time of which God had spoken to him. (Genesis 21:2)

And the Lord appointed a set time, saying, tomorrow the Lord shall do this thing in the land. (Exodus 9:5)

For the vision is yet for an appointed time, but at the end it shall speak, and not lie; though it tarry, come, it will not tarry. (Habakkuk 2:3)

Job said, "all of my appointed time shall I wait until my change come." (Job 14:14)

Solomon said, there is a time for everything. (Job 3:1)

David said, "Hide me in thy wrath and remember me at the appointed time." (Job 14:13)

God calls it divine timing and an appointed time.

Without divine timing, life's events will run into each other, showing up at the wrong time in our lives. Timing is important for preparation.

- Enter into his rest.

- Wait for your appointed time.

- Cast your cares on him.

- Have confidence in the direction God is taking your life.

- Walk in his liberty.

Jesus knew he came from above. Jesus used to always talk about where he was going. He told the disciples, "You can't go where I'm going." It's the same for us.

God will reveal parts of our future to us also. He is going to manifest himself to you if you keep his commandments because he is our friend and he wants us to know that he is still alive.

His spirit will give you the confidence that He is your father. That is why we cry Abba (our) Father. This causes us to feel related to him. I don't worry about anything that happens because I have experienced God as my Father and because his spirit confirmed with my spirit that I am his child. I could feel the adoption going through. Nothing will separate me from his love. He knows me.

Get to know God for yourself. It has to be a personal experience—you know, between you and God. I experienced him as my personal Savior, and my spirit was reborn. I took on his very nature. Jesus is Lord to the glory of God the Father. You must experience him the same way. Ask him into your heart and to be the Lord of your life. What you experience will never be forgotten. This experience cannot be gained in any other way. Most important is that hearing from God for yourself removes doubt that he is alive, and the direction for your life will actually come from him.

Prayer is the time to get to know the God of my deliverance. I commune with him daily, so I can receive messages from him as I learn to hear. I recommend you start with a morning prayer. The morning, I think, has a certain preparedness for the day. You will begin to hear that still voice inside you. You do have to develop an ear to hear, but it will come with spirituality born out of keeping his commandments.

Jesus promised that his sheep know his voice. He spoke directly to me when he gave me instruction. Or actually, maybe the words were written on my mind. I can never figure out sometimes how God did it. There are other voices out there sent from the pit to confuse us, but you will always recognize his voice. But you have to read about him and get to know him intimately so you are known by him.

The heavenly Father requires that you accept Jesus Christ as your Lord and Savior. If you do this, you are instantly entitled to all of the blessings under the New Testament covenant, including the freedom to walk in his liberty. Continue, in the meantime, to enjoy his liberty, until suddenly, one day you find the time to get to good ground has expired.

God commands angels that are dispatched and are encamped around you. This is to protect and keep us safe. God dispatches them. They too will advise you, if you depend on God. I was so depressed once I could not clean my house. An angel girl (in a female's voice) told me to clean my house. I was so depressed, but I got up and started cleaning my house anyway. Walk in the liberty by which Christ has made you free. I chose to clean to be in the habit of obeying the voice of

God's representatives, much like Joseph did when the angel told him to take the child and his mother and flee because there were those who sought to kill him (Matthew 2:13).

PART III

CHAPTER 5

Sally/Case Study

I remember being a little girl the first time I felt this inner loneliness. I just know it was always there. Was I born with it? I would spend most of my life trying to fill it—my inner void.

I couldn't understand what was happening. My house was surrounded by officers of the law and their police cruisers parked at odd angles all over the street, and they were there for me. Why did the marshal say I tried to kill him? The gun wasn't pointed at him. Now I had the marshal and the police, and an ambulance had just arrived. I was surrounded the landlord and of course the onlookers—cats, dogs, birds, and squares in my face at my front door. My world was crashing in on me. God, not the papers—please don't let this make the papers. *Why are they taking me to the hospital?* I thought.

Long before that part of my life I will never forget I was lying on the couch. My mother walked through the front door, and I jumped up. Nobody could lay around the house after 8:00 a.m. no matter what day it was. She told me to get up and go to the Westly Niles Library because Roman Ward was hiring. He was the project director for a program to transition college-level students with business backgrounds into professional positions.

My name is Sally, by the way. I was born and raised in Kyle, Texas, twenty minutes outside of Austin. Kyle is the home of the pie in Texas. I worked at a private college in Kyle for many years.

If I had to be addicted to drugs, thank God it didn't happen while my mother was alive, although I believe the dead do know.

Like most addicts, I had so much going for myself. I remember pleading the case of my innocence to God. I was angry, and I just wanted to know what path this was. How could I end up on drugs? I told God, "I've been with you since I was eleven years old. You didn't look out for me. You didn't protect me. I would rather have stayed in eternity than have been brought to a life of addiction."

I want to share how my heavenly Father dealt with my addiction, which is how he will deal with you.

But first, there were some good times and memorable times at home growing up.

My mother was the glue that held the family together. She was that kind of mommy who got up every morning and helped you get dressed for school, gave you your vitamins, and made breakfast. She always gave me and my siblings the best Christmases, Thanksgivings, and Easters, making four Easter baskets faithfully every year, and then there were the New Years. We were always in church on New Year's. That's how we celebrated.

But every Christmas, we each had a shot of Mogen David wine. That was a childhood family tradition in our house.

I bonded with God early in life. I prayed continually. The greatest gift my mother gave to me was introducing me to God. My mother would have me and my brothers kneel and bow our knees and lead us in the Lord's Prayer, teaching it to us. I loved God in those days, and I could feel his love. I had great aspirations for us because I knew he would be a part of my life always.

I remember liking life as an adolescent. My mother found this little church through which God would forge his presence in my life. I was about eleven, and I belonged to a secret club for young girls.

The bishop's sisters, Mary and Etta, would teach us different crafts. We sold our merchandise at the church bazaar. They taught us to be ladies, and I wanted to be just like them.

I sang in the choir when I was a young teen. There were times when life was fun.

I belonged to my church choir, and we would travel to different churches and events on the outskirts of Austin and sing, and families at the different churches would have us all over for dinner. I remember thinking how special I felt for someone to have us all over as a group for such a fine dinner. And I saw how well other people lived. And I enjoyed singing for the Lord and living for him too.

As I became older, the church formed a baseball team. My family, along with other families, was picked up for the games in the church van. How wholesome was that? I used to wonder what they would do if they only knew a real life boogeyman was driving the church van.

I'd graduated from high school and had two years of college on a part-time basis. I was working in my fallback career working for a private college twenty minutes outside of Austin. The other secretaries and I would meet in the parking lot in one of our cars, and we passed the pills. They made us type faster. We typed letters, reports, research papers, requisitions, exams (some eighty question or more), minutes, you name it. That is when I started experimenting with pills, but that was a short stint. It's also where I would be in my career for the next seventeen years, too afraid to trust the gifts God planted in me. My heart dreamed to be a writer.

I was working seven hours, forty-five minutes a day and then getting high after work. That left me with two options—either cook something to eat or get two hours of sleep before having to get up for work. I opted for the sleep.

Can you imagine my horror when my boss, Dr. Katz, told me the faculty meeting was about me?

The faculty want to know why I lost so much weight and if I was ill. It seems my skeletal remains looked rather ghostly.

After my last promotion and a new supervisor, something had to come to an end, I suppose. The Human Resources Department was doing a six-month time and attendance review on me. I took a leave to go to rehab and relapsed hours after my release. This new doctor, Dr. Judith Wiessman, my new supervisor, was relentless in her quest to rid everyone of me once and for all. I should have seen it coming. She would have me terminated at any cost. She started falsifying my timesheet. I would fill it out and sign it and submit it to her for her signature, and she would take her big, fat, red pen and write over my writing a later time than when I came in, literally falsifying my time sheet. No one would hear me when I told them she was doing this. I was eventually terminated. That was how bad she wanted me out. I had borrowed against my retirement and didn't pay it back before I left.

Shortly after that, an eviction from my drug den (apartment) followed.

It was, however, determined that I was not going to shoot the marshal, but perhaps a stay at the hospital might be better suited for me.

So, I was jobless and homeless at the same time with no place to sleep. Eventually help did arrive. I will just say a Good Samaritan gave me a place to lodge until I could find a way to get back on my feet.

Even though I was raised in the church and sang in the choir, I tried marijuana when I was sixteen. And in my twenties, I was trying pills and cocaine and then crack approximately by age thirty-four. Here I would remain for years to come.

I tried crack, the most addictive of the top ten addictive drugs, and that was all it took before an addiction burst forth. Every area of my life became an unmanageable nightmare. My career would suffer the most, or maybe it was the credit. With drugs, every area of your life gets destroyed at once, and it's worse the more addictive the drug. So with addiction, you don't get one shut-off notice. Every company is threatening lawsuits or to terminate services. I prayed, "Why, God? When I was young, I idolized you. Or why couldn't you just leave me where I was: in eternity?"

What had I done as a child or in eternity that I should end up addicted to crack? I wanted to know how he could let this devastating addiction happen to me. Me, whom he formed in my mother's womb, whom he did predestinate. I actually used to think about what God's explanation to me would be because I was angry and embarrassed about my life.

I felt like one of the disciples when he asked of God, "Whose sin caused this man to be born blind? Was it his parents?" I was wondering whose sin was visited upon me.

I was a Christian struggling with addiction. I remember realizing in church I was not hearing any teaching about Jesus delivering anyone from drugs or anyone having an addiction. But in all the Hollywood movies, all the pharaohs and kings always drank wine. They partied at dinner every night, so they must have been winos. The church did not seem to have the language or scripture to cover the subject of addiction. So it was okay to go to meetings where sobriety was being taught. My pastor had no problem with my going. Sobriety was the focus, but spirituality was also encouraged.

I remember when it happened for me. Out of the clear blue, I was truly set free. I was set free from crack cocaine. The habit just left me. It can be extremely baffling when it happens. I told everyone that the addiction just left me and I was never going to use again. It was finally over. I remember wondering about the power that suddenly freed me. What was it, and where did it come from? It was simply a miracle. One minute I had an addiction problem, and the next minute the urge to use vanished.

All I wanted to do was recover everything I lost in addiction. I wanted my credit rating back. I wanted to get rid of that cloud of addiction that swirled around me. I wanted to be that person people looked up to again. I was striving for that. I set out to do it on my own because I couldn't trust God. I thought he was going to cause me to miss out on opportunities or be slow to tell me how to act or if I should act at all or wait and then the opportunity is gone. And I hate it when I seek him in prayer and I get silence for an answer! But I firmly believe now that if God is not answering, more patience and preparation are needed. Or perhaps, do not proceed.

I was clean for six months. Then, one day out of the clear blue, the urge to use came back. I relapsed. I was dumbfounded. Why, Lord? Was it because I went to the bar? But I didn't drink. (A friend of mine owned a bar.) It was a hangout place to say hello where everybody really did know your name.

I had missed my opportunity to be with God, and I didn't even know it. When God's liberty fell upon me, I was free with the power of choice to choose him, but instead I chose to do it the world's way. When God took his liberty away from me, I was vulnerable to the forces that be and the urge to use. The addiction spirits were back, and they pounced all over me.

I was neither hot nor cold; I was lukewarm. I was friends with the world and God. God spit me out of his mouth. His spirit no longer dwelled in me. I was weak. I relapsed.

God spit me out of his mouth. Don't be lukewarm. He wants us to seek true riches—to be like him. But also, he wants us to dream our biggest dreams so he can bring these good works out of us. These good works are his will.

The other problem I had trying to stay clean was that I really didn't know how to surrender. I grew up in the church, but I didn't know how to surrender. I guess I could not wrap my mind around the fact that a God in the heavens was actually going to reach down into my life and communicate with me about the goings on in my personal life.

But once the cycle of addiction kicked in, it took me another seven years to get clean again.

The fear of relapsing was always there. There was always that fear. I know the pain of not wanting to tell anyone you've been set free because you are afraid you might relapse or no one will believe you anyway. We were relapsing because we were doing it our way. I didn't realize I could not do it without him. I did not trust that God could actually communicate to me the direction for my life and his will in it. I did not set out to exclude God, but I did not believe he could truly direct my life from heaven. And I did not have the patience to wait on his answers to my prayers. I forgot about God and to consider him and his ways. Besides, my liberation from drugs was so blissful that I really felt I could manage the rest of my life on my own. I was happy. I thought that if I could just get rid of the drugs, that was all I needed to become a star. But like the other addicts who relapsed, I forgot just how cunning the drugs are without God.

It would take many years and finally learning how to surrender before I would finally stop relapsing.

When God decided to call me out of my addiction, he planted sobriety like a dream come true in my heart. I pleaded with God to give me another chance at sobriety. This time he did not give me instant sobriety. He gave me an appointed time. I almost suffered a heart attack, and I got an appointed time! I could not believe it. He gave me an appointed time. I had to wait on God and stay focused on him. I even hoped my appointed time would come before my appointment with death. The Lord kept echoing to me, *"You can do nothing without me"* *(John 5:15).* I wanted to be free from drugs at any cost, so I was patient, and at the appointed time, God did set me free. I received his liberty and my sobriety.

I was driven to take the power from this addiction demon by exposing the evil and identifying it. The control and the force with which it took over my life, resources, and relationships was extraordinary. The most plaguing fear was always, "Will the urge to use ever be gone for good? Could it really be over?" It was like fighting a living, breathing, invisible spirit person, which could think on its own, and I hoped at times it couldn't read my thoughts. If that sounds scary to you, I was living it.

When I was finally ready to do it his way, this is the message he gave me:

> *A sower went out to sow his seed; and as he sowed, some fell by the wayside; and it was trodden down and the fowls of the air devoured it. And some fell upon a rock; and as soon as it was sprung up, it withered away, because it lacked moisture. And some fell among thorns, and the thorns sprang up with it, and choked it. And others fell on good ground, and sprang up, and bore fruit and hundredfold. And when he had said these things, he cried, he that hath ears to hear, let him hear. And his disciples asked him, saying what might this parable be? And he said, "Unto you it is given to know the mysteries of the kingdom of God,*

> *but others I use parables, that seeing they*
> *might not see, and hearing they might not*
> *understand." Now the parable is this. The*
> *seed is the word of God. Those by the way*
> *side are they that hear; then cometh the*
> *devil, and taketh away the word out of*
> *their hearts, lest they should believe and*
> *be saved. (Luke 8:5–12)*

To you former addicts standing by the wayside, God has included you in his liberty. But you prefer the pursuit of your own worldly, tainted riches rather than trusting God to bring forth riches from you. People and spirits in the air are poised to root out your liberty lest it take root. God allowed his liberty to find you, but standing by the wayside are your new friends and old friends; smiling faces are at the ready to prevent knowledge of him from taking hold.

> *They on the rock are they whom, when they hear, receive*
> *the word with joy; and these have no root, who for a while*
> *believe, and in time of testing fall away. (Luke 8:13)*

These are those who, when addicted, received God's mercy and received his liberty and pursued for a while but never were grounded in the word. When trouble comes, they feel God has deserted them, so they fall away and relapse, never having matured. Being far from the word, they lack moisture. Consequently, their life is not set up for Christian living.

> *And that which fell among thorns are they who, when they have heard, go forth, and are choked with the cares and riches and pleasures of this life, and bring no fruit to perfection. (Luke 8:14)*

To those of you who prefer the riches of the world instead of the dreams God has planted in you, you have chosen against God's will. I implore you, if it is riches you desire, enter into his will, and your life will turn different corners until you reach riches stored up. When you want to do a thing, think and decide if it is a direction you desire to go or according to the word if this is the direction God would want for you. You must follow your spirit and go with the truth in every case. He wants to pluck prosperity from you. Not doing it God's way, using the channels and people he will work through, puts you on a different path than him. And then the work in the spiritual is not brought to perfection because you've done things your way. The last thing I need is to struggle, so I am going to allow him to direct my path.

Being caught up in the pleasures of this world will surely cause one to relapse.

> *But that on the good ground are they who,*
> *in an honest and good heart having heard*
> *the word, keep it and bring forth fruit with*
> *patience. (Luke 8:5–15)*

These are men and women who, when God called them out of addiction, gladly made him the head of their lives and are bringing forth good fruit in the form of good works. God is pruning them and getting them ready for their next assignments. They are always prospering, helping the people around them and in their communities.

Addicts all over the world dream of the day when they will be drug free.

God is sowing his liberty too in the lives of men and women who want to be set free. When we ask God to free us from addiction, he has an appointed time when he will do it. No one knows when an appointed time will arrive until it shows up. People are suddenly being set free, and it is because their appointed time has arrived and God is answering their cries and their prayers. We who he sets free are standing on different ground than another set free. But we all must get to good ground. You and I have to recognize we must get to good ground and make God the head of our lives when we are set free because, when he sets us free, he gives us also our power of choice to freely choose him, so we have no excuse.

I had to ask myself what ground was I standing. When God extended his liberty to me and took the power of addiction from the drug so when I heard the mention of the word I was not triggered and he gave me power of choice, I too had to get to good ground. No one knows the day or hour when God's liberty will arrive or on what ground it will find you. But when liberty found me, I went to good ground. So now all of his blessings will find me on good ground.

If you want to part take in his liberty, abide in his word and allow his Spirit to abide in you. You will be made free, and he will pluck good works from you. Don't fall into the "I don't know what to do with my time rut; I have all this idle time now." Start your good works or the works in your personal life that you know need to be taken care of.

God is planting his liberty in the hearts of addicts all over the world. These are addicts who hate what they do and are not able to perform that which is good. It is up to God how he deals with us individually.

- There are times God wields his liberty and addicts are set free at the very moment—restoring them in the spirit of their mind, soul, heart, and character.

- Other times he plants his liberty in the hearts of addicts all over the world, like a dream come true, calling them out of their addiction and to his attention. (These begin to seek him and dream of life without addiction.)

- And yet, to another he gives an appointed time and one has to stay focused on God, praying diligently, fighting the good fight of faith, believing that at the appointed time God will remember to set him free.

God may require one to suffer all of the above steps.

In the meantime, I like to recommend the online study tools, (visual bible, online bible, and the online research material and speakers) as well as support groups. Get a support group, go to meetings and church meetings, and wait on the Lord by occupying all of your time, staying busy and always prayerful. If you don't get instant sobriety, there are parts of every addict's day when they are not feeling the urge to use. Yes, it is true. You might have an addiction, but you are not addicted twenty-four hours in a day. There are parts of your day where you are able to function outside of your addiction. The cravings and triggers happen sometime during the day. That part of your day that your addiction has not kicked in is when you have to be the most productive. That time should be strategically scheduled, especially remembering to meditate in prayer. This can happen anywhere you are. That time of each day should be spent taking care of your personal business and your affairs, remembering to meditate on his word and go to a group where sobriety and faith in God are taught.

My sobriety suddenly showed up for me, although I had been praying and believing for it. So one day I got an application for a credit card in the mail. I wanted this card, but I didn't want to start taking forty-dollar intervals of cash out the ATM to feed an addiction. I had just filed for bankruptcy. What should I do? Was the addiction going to hijack the card, or should I just not get the card and wait?

Well, I decided to apply for the card. One Sunday evening at 6:00 p.m., I applied over the phone; she ran my application and said, "Congratulations! You've been approved." At the sound of the word *approved*, my addiction left me. I have not seen it since.

This liberty granted to graft addicts in or we would perish in our addictions. We get freedom from drugs accompanied with the power to choose. I made the decision right then and there to forget about my desires and allow his will to be my will. Having taken the path God laid out for my life has left me in a position better than I could have ever imagined—certainly better than I could have accomplished on my own.

You can receive God's liberty no matter on what ground it finds you. But you have a window to get to good ground where you can be safe from relapse and where life is good and plentiful. If you don't get there, a place where you allow God to pluck good works from you, you could end up in a corner relapsed. Either way, you will be miserable and dying. When you delight yourself in the things of the Lord, he will give you the desires of your heart. This is good ground.

When you seek the kingdom of God and all of its righteousness, all of these other things will be added unto to you. This is good ground.

The Lord is my shepherd, and I shall not want. This is good ground.

Have you ever felt agape love? God's love. This is good ground.

The first time I tasted God's liberty, I was standing on thorny ground—yeah, definitely on thorny ground. But I live and breathe on good ground now.

I live on good ground. I make all my decisions there. Good ground is the only ground where you can resist the devil and where he will flee. The reason the devil will flee is because good ground is being connected on the vine with God so his Spirit lives in you and directs you. My confidence is greatly increased because life is good. The parmagrant trees; the olive trees; grapevines and fig trees are all flourishing and there is enough oil and wine for a lifetime.

The Spirit is the Lord. Where the Lord is, there is liberty. God will strengthen me in my spirit man because that is where I am one with him. Addiction cannot survive here on good ground because it has nothing to feed upon.

God wants to direct my life to the abundant riches he has for me, which is why he planted sobriety like a dream in my heart. Some dreams can only be achieved by accessing God. You can regain everything you lost in addiction, according to God's good pleasure. It happened for me. God set a table for me and made me lie down in green pastures, and he restored my soul. When you lie down in green pastures, you won't want to get up. It feels marvelous.

PART IV

CHAPTER 6

We Are the Branches, He Is the Gardener

God the Father chastens every one of his children that he loves. This correction brings with it spiritual maturity and wisdom from God. And every branch in God that bears good fruit he prunes and rids the branch of dead growth. That gets it ready for more fruit so the new fruit can come forth easily.

God our Father is the Gardener, and we are the branches rooted in Jesus, the vine. God will cut the dead branches (people) from the vine that do not bear good fruit. These deprive the good branches of their nourishment by taking away oxygen and water. Each of us are here to perform a service that God has planted in us. Jesus nourishes the branches and shines on us until we understand our work, how to proceed, and with whom to work or to work alone. Then the sun shines on our dreams and they flourish. So let us hear from him so our fruit, dreams, and works will come to fruition and succeed.

After addiction, we have to leave the old life behind to move beyond addiction. God wants to do more than kill our addiction. He taught me to trust him and not the economy or modern-day technology or my jobs but to trust in him who upholds the universe by his word. He wants you to learn of his truth and grace and trust him too.

God the Father wants to cut away everything that is not like him. He will prune the branches of everything in us that is not like him—bad habits, cheating, stubbornness, I could go on.

We have to continue to be renewed in our spirit minds through our relationship with the Comforter. God is going to strengthen us in our spirit man. No more lying, stealing, filthy talk, and jesting. No fornication or scheming should be a part of our lives. He will give us his very nature, which is love, peace, patience, and longsuffering. He wants us to be sober minded, and we will want to do his will.

After God has freed us, we have a responsibility to God to work. We are obligated by our marriage to him to bring forth fruit. We are here to bear good fruit unto God. I want to be fruitful. I am married to him and am required to bring forth fruit, which is his kingdom work. We are to be fruitful and multiply in our works. We are not to be lazy but productive. We all have gifts and talents and are inspired and so have to walk the path God has called each of us to. I want to be productive to get back what was stolen in addiction. I long to bring forth good fruit. Any person who does not bear good fruit will wither and die. That means find what makes you happy and flourish in it. So I will find whatever I can do, of course, that God would want me to do, and of course, something that I am capable of doing and be productive in it. I learned to process the world through the inner man and follow his lead. Inactivity can cause various health issues too. For one, you lower your respirations, and eventually you forget to breathe. And why sit around wasting every day? Ask God for an idea. This is what God wants us to do. So don't say, "Now that I'm clean, I don't know what to do with my time, my life, or my day." God is expecting us to do something productive. We must pull our own weight now that we are clean and always be in a position to help someone, if they need it. That is the way it is with God. When you follow his instructions and follow your spirit, you have enough resources left over to help someone.

For we who depend on God and live on good ground, God prepares more and more fruit in our lives to come forth until we are full of abundance. We have works and projects to accomplish and we need to complete them.

If you do not use your liberty to help others, you go against his will for your life. We are here to serve. You will be chopped from the vine. He will allow you to go off on your own path, and the fruit you bring forth will have blemishes on it and will not be perfect.

Jesus talked about spirits that work in the children of disobedience. He said in past times we were fulfilling the desires of the flesh and of the mind.

Crack cocaine is one of those desires of the mind. It hijacks the brain's normal function and turns the brain into a computer rigged to only want pleasure from using at the expense of death.

The reason I was relapsing and other addicts weren't is because there was no relationship with the only power that can break the power of addiction. I either did not know how to or was unwilling to surrender my will.

Jesus taught me to trust him and to be patient, and he cut away everything that is not like him. I started seeing my dreams actually happening, and you will too, if you are patient and are willing to bring forth good fruit and work on it every day until you make it happen.

So dream your biggest and wildest dreams because you can ask whatsoever you want as long as you keep his commandments. And he has promised to perform it.

When I relapsed, it was because I produced no fruit. When Jesus was hungry and the fig tree had produced no figs, he cursed that fig tree because it was not fulfilling its purpose. Before my name was Sally, God planted in me good fruit that he wants me to bring forth, and in you also is planted fruit. Whom he did know before the foundation of the world he did also predestinate. God planted in all of us all kinds of gifts and talents so we are equipped to carry out his will on earth. I've learned to respect the paths of others because we all have our own path in his will to travel.

When standing on good ground, the fruits God wants to bring forth in us are our gifts and talents that he planted in us but also every unexpected work he would have me to do. I've been apprehensive at times about doing the work I'm called to do or investing time and money, but to be in the will of God, I had to do what God required of me and execute his will. Walk in the liberty of your calling. When you trust God and take that first step, he will be there to guide you and open up the vision.

It is the same way God restored Job. Remember, in the book of Job, Job lost his children, his cattle, and his riches, and he was ill. God gave Job another family and more cattle than he had before, and everyone lived in a new house. And Job was healed of his terrible illness.

The same way God restored Job's life, he propelled me from being a lodger to lady of the manor.

In my opinion, God plants in us the type of man or woman we are to be attracted to also. This is so we have harmony with our spouse as we carry out his will on earth and also so our spouse will be supportive in our work that we are called to. So take the time to look for the qualities in a mate you are attracted to because every man is not for every woman and every woman is not for every man. Look for the person looking for you and your qualities. Make sure that man or woman is God's will for your life, first. Again this is only my opinion.

CHAPTER 7

Walk in the Liberty ...

God's liberty is holy because he is holy. To walk in his liberty is the freedom to do his will. That does not mean he is going to have you parting the sea in the middle of the desert—unless that is the liberty you are called to. Doing his will can be as simple as going out of your way a little to help someone. Or for example, if you have organizational skills and can write grants, you may open a pantry to help families in the neighborhood. It is that radiant light in you that shines when you are doing good works that people can see, letting your light shine wherever you are in life and in the world. His will is his word and anything he lays on your heart to do. When I apply his word to my daily living, I am choosing to walk in his liberty. I'm endeavoring to become good soil for him if he's going to plant his seed so he can pluck good fruit from me and bring forth good works.

I will serve the Lord because I want his will for me. I want the dreams he planted in me and the surprise gifts from God I never see coming that he provides to me because he is my heavenly Father and he loves me and wants me to prosper. So why would I want to do it my way? My way led to an addiction. But I'm free now.

It is a new start for me and I do have to say, I love myself whom God has set free. When God is at the head of our lives, he will teach us to trust him, how to have patience, and he will increase our wisdom. I realized I am making the best decisions over my life. You will learn to depend on him and make the best decisions also.

Sometimes, though, I feel as though I am in the desert while I wait on God. I try to enjoy the other parts of my life but still function in all areas and continue to be patient. I try not to complain too much while I wait, but I have a ways to go.

As we walk in our vocation or whatever work we believe we are called to do, we fulfill his divine plan and his will becomes our will. Sometimes fear may come to mind, but fear is a spirit. God did not give us the spirit of fear, so go out on that limb and trust God. That is what he is calling us to do.

The benefits are abundance and having the desires of our hearts met. It's a blissful feeling. I am expecting the desires of my heart and nothing less because he wants us to prosper, and I would like that as well. So I walk in the direction of the calling in me.

So, here I am writing my story for the body of Christ for those who are suffering an addiction, as I once suffered. As I write these words, I have no idea what direction God will take my life. What I know is that I can rest in him and be at peace.

Can you imagine a father who can give you sobriety, wisdom, a million-dollar idea, good health, a solution to your problems—whatever you can think of? When

God gave me sobriety, he revealed himself to me concerning my work. So I am stepping out on faith and walking in his liberty to bring it to pass. I am glad I have a mind to write and enjoy what I'm doing at the same time. It was his liberty that set me free and made it possible. His will is my will because I always wanted to be an author.

I needed God's direction. You have that same power of choice that Jesus wields. You can create and live your life and have fun, too. Go to lunch with your friends or take a trip around the world. Do whatever you want, on good ground.

If you need more help in your personal life, *"he is a rewarder of them who diligently seek him" (Hebrews 11:6).* If you want to access the big blessings God has to offer, if you want to obtain them and hold on to them, go after what God has planted in your heart to do. He gave it for you. If you want God to back your dreams, go after his will. He wants his will done on earth. Make his will your will and your dream, and I guarantee you he will be at the helm until your dream is achieved!

No matter how many years you spend in addiction, when you get on the path God has for you, when he feels so moved, our Father has presents for you too. You might get a dream come true, like the trip you always wanted, but my experience has been the desire of my heart or a blessing I never saw coming. But expect to learn some lessons, expect to mature while you wait on God, and expect God to prune your branches. The key is to stay busy while you wait.

When I am in my vehicle or standing in a bank line or a grocery line, I pray and meditate on his word. As you pray, meditate on the scripture that you need God to make come to life for you. I need someone to love. I did meet quite the man too. I meditate on the scripture in the book of Plasm that reads, "I am my beloved and my beloved is mine." This has yet to be fulfilled, though.

When God reveals to you how he is going to bless your life, remember to always stay on good ground, and when you can't go any further in your endeavors or dreams, wait. Wait for the people and opportunities God has for you. God, who sees the whole picture, will definitely be there because he will never leave you, but you might feel like your faith is being tried.

When the time is right, God will order your steps. One day, all of a sudden it was like a weight lifted off my mind and I knew it was time to make a decision and go forward with the project. The time was right, and my spirit knew to prompt me to go ahead and commit. Wait for the people and opportunities God has for you. When you feel you've done everything and you don't know what else to do, maybe it's time to wait.

When God showed me part of my future, I immediately trusted by preparing for my future and incorporating it into my current life as much as I could. You must live your dream and make it a part of you, a part of your psyche, so that in God's divine timing, everything will fall into place.

I think about Jesus. He always knew where he was going. He talked about it too. He knew he came from above. He told the disciples, "You can't go where I am going." He had a purpose every day too. Jesus told them the Comforter could not come until he went away.

The Holy Spirit knows all things, and he will tell you things about your future too. When we do the work we are called to do, it could possibly be the turning point in life we need—our new direction.

I know a little about where I am going, as revealed by God, and nothing will interfere with God's plan for my life because I want it too badly.

When you get clean from drugs, you will need patience. You need patience because all the players in your affairs have to be in place; you may need a level of wisdom that God needs to mature you to. And when it's time to act, God will enlighten your mind and you will know it is time to act, make a decision, commit, or whatever the case may be—that is, if you don't become impatient and do things your selfish way instead of God's way.

Consider for a moment King David when he was a boy. When Samuel anointed David and told him he would be king of Israel, David didn't become king until many, many years later.

When Job lost everything, it took many years for his change to come.

Noah was ridiculed for building the ark. But he worked on that ark every day. He lived what God told him and he built the ark by making it a part of his life every day. That is a perfect example of how Noah walked in God's liberty. He had freedom to do God's will and had no addiction tormenting his mind. Choose to walk in the vocation and then start fulfilling the duties you're called to do. That is how Noah obeyed and prepared for the flood God told him would come. And God did not forget to send the flood.

You may come to a standstill in your work you're called to do. That is okay. Remember patience. Wait on God, but while you wait, do all the preparation so when God orders your steps, you are ready.

Beloved, move and work in the direction of your calling. If you don't know what direction, look inside yourself. What do you like to do? What can you do? What is at your disposal for you to do? God has a way of giving you a mind to know what to do and what direction to go in, if you depend on him.

He didn't forget to make David king. He didn't forget to send the flood when he told Noah to build the ark. He didn't forget to raise Jesus from the dead.

I want the abundance Jesus told me was mine and nothing less because I am an heir of God and a joint heir with Christ. It's mine because he is the Lord of my life and I keep his commandments.

There are times I want to step out on my own, but he keeps me. I am fearful that I might miss the best God has for me. God has shown me some of my future, and it is better than anything I could accomplish on my own.

His spirit will commune with your spirit, and you will want to be like him. You are going to become conscious of his ways and will want to imitate them. It is communing with God that helps one to stay on good ground. Walk in God's liberty.

Addiction has no authority over us. We hold this power of choice. Christ's liberty is holy, and we are connected to him by his spirit so our actions are holy. (If you make a mistake, repent as soon as possible.)

Realize your new life without drugs and feel how glorious the sun feels. Now start to fulfill the dreams God is awakening in you.

Walk in God's freedom from drugs by choosing to keep his commandments and you will be choosing his liberty and the new life he is directing you toward. Continue to confide in him so he can reveal his path for your life, and take everything to him in prayer. And do not be afraid to walk in the direction he is leading you.

Examine your dreams and your heart, and see what God has planted for you. You will be truly excited for the first time in a long time. Don't be afraid to pursue your dreams.

God's liberty is holy because he is holy. I choose to live in his will for my life, exercising my freedom to choose what is acceptable to him. That is the same power of choice Jesus wielded when he shone his presence on me and made me free from drugs because one cannot describe just how the miracle happens.

To choose this liberty, I must choose the behavior that God has preordained that I walk in. When you choose his will, you begin to experience the excitement of the new foundation he is building in your new life.

Nothing is as wonderful as having your mind restored to have freedom to live and choose. Addiction has no more rule over us. I choose Christ, where liberty lives. Incidentally, I like God's will for my life. Walking in or choosing his liberty is choosing his will for my life.

Aligning my life with his is key. Then you will begin to hear from God concerning your personal life.

Follow the instruction of God for your life. Just as Jesus told the disciples to go to the seashore, take the coin out of the fish's mouth, and pay his taxes and the others' taxes, he will give you the same answers you need for your life, if you trust him and depend on him and keep his commandments. You can receive instruction from God for your life too.

I didn't have to guess what direction God wanted me to travel. When you hear from God, you will know and won't doubt it is him. If you need reassurance from God, ask him to increase your faith. Walk in this liberty.

I used to wonder all my life, how do I get to the abundant life God has for me! Hello, God, can you just tell me that? I can remember praying to God many times, saying, "Lord, I am on the down side of my life, and I have a history of drug abuse." I would ask the Lord, "How can this work together for my good?" You said, "All things work together for the good of them who love God."

When you incorporate God's plans—his teaching and instructions from the word—into your daily life, it is a blessed feeling because that new road begins to open new doors and old doors are closed. You can see the changes happening. God will inspire you and you will know you are walking in the liberty he called you to. You will feel amazed at how God is literally leading you and changing your life and destiny. There is no guesswork. You will feel his joy.

I started dreaming my wildest and biggest dreams addiction robbed me of. The talents God has given me, along with his inspiration, are being invested in the body of Christ. I am doing the work he has called me to do. Good works produce good fruit. You will feel his inspiration throughout this book.

It is my desire through my work that others will be inspired in their relationship with God and will want to know him better.

God will give us the vision, and we are to do the physical work and planning to manifest it. Walk in this liberty. Through this process, God will bring forth good fruit in our lives. Walk in his liberty and let your light shine. You will begin to feel like your old self again, and "he will restore your soul."

Walk in your vocation. Whatever work God has put on your heart to do, you must begin to incorporate it into your daily life. Set the time aside and do the work, even if it is thirty minutes a day.

I didn't know how to write or structure a book, but as I started working, God opened up the vision, and I could see how to proceed.

When God is directing you, he will give you directions when it is time, so you don't become overwhelmed. Those who are recently clean, your obedience to walk as God has called you could be the only thing saving you from relapsing.

I remembered my dreams even when I played with Barbie dolls as a little girl. I started thinking about the talents God planted in me—what I like to do. I always wanted to be a writer. I used to dream of being a writer by profession, married to an executive. Whatever my dreams, God planted dreams in all of our hearts, and he gave us talents to fulfill them. We can realize dreams at different phases throughout our lives. We only have to keep dreaming and keep our faith and know we are the beloved of God, and he will help us fulfill our dreams.

This is a turning point. Walk in your vocation. All over the globe God is raising up people he has delivered out of every situation that impacts man's relationship with him to be an example to the body of Christ. This is God being a very present help. Your life experiences can benefit humankind.

As you wait for God to bring about and direct you to different experiences in your life, there are things you can do to set a tone of excellence by living a life that will bode well for your future.

One of the largest obstacles I was faced with was having a lot of time and no patience. Time is a large obstacle for those who no longer spend time using. That time has to be restructured. You have to learn to live with yourself—spend time alone. Make a list of all the things you said you were going to do when you stopped using. Then start doing the things on your list. I got an animal. When the Lord delivered me from drugs, the Lord told me to clean up my debt. I decided to take this a step further, so I established excellent credit. Walk in this liberty. I exercised my freedom of choice and obeyed God's instructions for my life. Overhaul your files and finances. Just stay busy and learn to spend time with yourself without complaining. Not that I don't complain.

But now, I try to be considerate of others. What about a ballroom dancing class?

As I tuned in to God during prayer, God revealed instructions to me disguised as ideas sometimes. I decided to do everything the correct way. I wanted to cut the negative ripple effect, be it on the earthly plane, cosmic plane, or otherwise.

My advice is that while you are waiting for God to reveal his path for your life, you can start to repair areas in your life that you have the total power to fix. Walk in this liberty by doing the following.

- Establish an excellent credit rating.

- Pay your monthly bills on time each month.

- Keep all of your doctor's and personal appointments

- Keep your house clean, and then clean the basement. Clean around your home, whether you rent or own.

- Don't miss work.

- If you wake up on Sunday and there are children in your home, go to church. Go to church anyway.

- Repair broken relationships, if possible.

- Spend time with your children.

- Develop a regular prayer life.

- Comply with whatever God has you to do.

- Eat healthy, well-rounded meals.

- Make and keep dental appointments.

- Develop a routine exercise program.

- Ask God to send you friends who love him who are free from addictions.

- Seek peace with all men.

These actions will empower you and increase your confidence. Anyone with an addiction problem for any period of time is aware that the above-listed are areas in every addict's life that have been neglected.

Don't be afraid to walk in his liberty. This will help you repair your life, and when you walk in Christ's liberty, the real person you are will come forth and shine. I took a stand to be a different person so my light could shine because I wanted to be that unique individual he has ordained me to be, and I want you to be that unique individual he ordained you to be.

When good goes out, good returns. When I started to pay my bills on time, keep my house clean, and find constructive things to do (like reading), I can honestly say life began to be kinder to me. I went from getting threating bill letters in the mail to credit card companies and banks and credit unions begging me to open accounts with them.

I realized it's not about my plan but God's direction for my life, and when you do the same, God will make you lie down in green pastures. This verse out of the book of Psalms will spring to life for you. It is a wonderful feeling to lie down in green pastures. That is the feeling of God's abundance. God will anoint your head with oil, and your cup will run over too. You need to experience what it feels like to the regain riches you lost in addiction. Then you will know what it feels like to lie down in green pastures.

If you stay connected to God on the vine, he will pour his spirit into yours and keep you clean and lead you even if an angel has to whisper in your ear. Remember, they are his messengers, and he will bring forth fruit in you—fruit he planted before you were born. Some gifts and talents are set like time capsules to come into fruition during certain periods in our lives. So look inside yourself and see what gifts he gave you, and perhaps you can find your start there. What are your dreams saying to you?

If we but dream our wildest dreams and believe, God will be there with us in the midst of our entire lives, bringing forth fruit in us that he planted to carry out his will. If you don't believe me, seek God for confirmation and see if he does not confirm to you that you are on the right path.

Don't be afraid. Be bold and confident. Your heavenly Father intervenes in the lives of his people.

It is key that we keep his commandments. I decided to be like Elizabeth, the mother of John the Baptist, and keep his ordinances as well.

Our higher power, Jesus, promises a personal visitation from him according to John 4:21. Expect him.

He said, *"He that hath my commandments, and keepeth them, he it is that loveth me, and he that loveth me shall be loved of my Father, and I will love him, and will manifest myself to him" (John 14:21).*

You see, he owes you a visit. That is a promise from God himself that he will pay each of us a visitation, and you will know he is alive. It is a supernatural experience. God almighty from heaven is signaling out you or me to communicate with in his supernatural way. I wish I could explain to you that kind of experience, but I can only experience it. I cannot explain it.

You can have everything you lost in your addiction restored to you, and more, if you would only dream your biggest dreams and depend on God to open up the vision for you and allow him to guide you to your blessings.

When I was addicted, I was not addicted twenty-four hours a day. The urge to use happens sometime during the day. When you are not feeling the urge to use, that is when you have to use the time wisely. I know there is a problem with motivation, but you will have to encourage yourself through the word and meditate on God's promises to you. Clean, wash, cook a good meal, or go out into the world and take care of your responsibilities. Use your good time wisely. Even plan how you will use this time. This you must do until your appointed time.

Please feel free to use this book as your personal study guide. You may mark your personal copy with a highlighter to reference parts that are important or specific to you or for any purpose you wish.

This book is dedicated to addicts all over the world who God is calling out of addiction—addicts who would do anything to have their power of choice restored so they can choose God.

Rest assured God wants to sow his liberty on you also.

CPSIA information can be obtained
at www.ICGtesting.com
Printed in the USA
BVHW070946240619
551797BV00007B/241/P